We're from Kenya

Emma Lynch

Heinemann Library
Chicago, Illinois

Customer Service 888-454-2279
Visit our website at www.heinemannlibrary.com

Editorial: Jilly Attwood, Kate Bellamy, Adam Miller
Design: Ron Kamen and Celia Jones
Picture research: Maria Joannou, Erica Newbery
Photographer: Roy Maconachie/EASI-Images
Production: Severine Ribierre

Originated by Ambassador Litho Ltd
Printed and bound in the United States, North Mankato, MN

12 11 10
10 9 8 7 6 5

Library of Congress Cataloging-in-Publication Data
Lynch, Emma.
  We're from Kenya / Emma Lynch.
     p. cm. -- (We're from)
  Includes bibliographical references and index.
  ISBN 1-4034-5806-5 (lib. bdg.) -- ISBN 1-4034-5815-4 (pbk.) 1. Kenya--Social life and customs--Juvenile literature. 2. Children--Kenya--Juvenile literature. 3. Family--Kenya--Juvenile literature. I. Title. II. Series.
  DT433.54.L95 2005
  967.6204'3--dc22
                                    2005002677

Acknowledgements
The publishers would like to thank the following for permission to reproduce photographs:
Audrius Tomonis p. **30c**; Corbis p. **30a**; Harcourt Education pp. **4, 5a, 5b, 6a, 6b, 7a, 7b, 8a, 8b, 9a, 9b, 10a, 10b, 11a, 11b, 12a, 12b, 13a, 13b, 14, 15a, 15b, 16a, 16b, 17a, 17b, 18a, 18b, 19a, 19b, 20, 21, 22, 23a, 23b, 24a, 24b, 25a, 25b, 26a, 26b, 27a, 27b, 28a, 28b, 29a, 29b, 30b** (Roy Maconachie/EASI-Images).

Cover photograph of Grace and her school friends, reproduced with permission of Harcourt Education Ltd/Roy Maconachie/EASI-Images.

Many thanks to Ronnie, Grace, Betty and Naomi, and their families. Our thanks also to Chris Waldron for his assistance in the preparation of this book.

Every effort has been made to contact copyright holders of any material reproduced in this book. Any omissions will be rectified in subsequent printings if notice is given to the publishers. The paper used to print this book comes from sustainable sources.

062010
Booksource

Contents

Some words are shown in bold, **like this**. You can find out what they mean by looking in the glossary.

Where Is Kenya?

To learn more about Kenya, we meet three children who live there. Kenya is a country in Africa. Kenya has the second highest mountain in Africa, Mount Kenya.

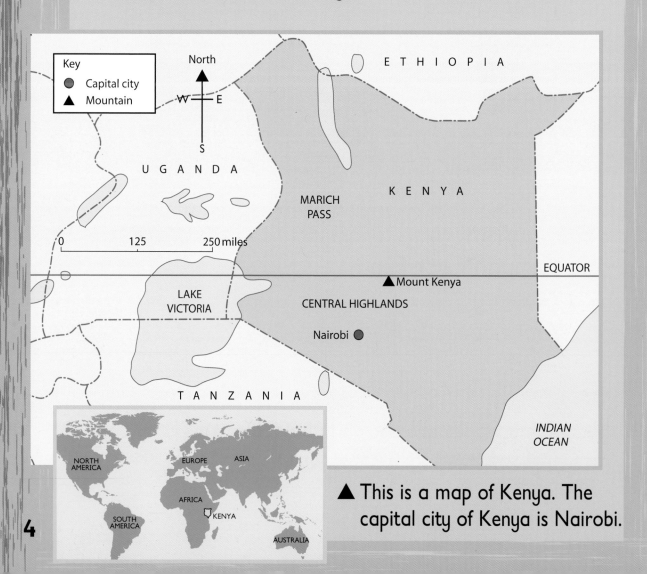

Key
- ● Capital city
- ▲ Mountain

North
W — E
S

ETHIOPIA

UGANDA

KENYA

MARICH PASS

0   125   250 miles

EQUATOR

LAKE VICTORIA

CENTRAL HIGHLANDS

▲ Mount Kenya

Nairobi ●

TANZANIA

INDIAN OCEAN

NORTH AMERICA
EUROPE   ASIA
AFRICA
KENYA
SOUTH AMERICA
AUSTRALIA

▲ This is a map of Kenya. The capital city of Kenya is Nairobi.

Kenya has low land near the sea. The weather here is **tropical**. Kenya has high land in the centre of the country. It is very dry in the high land.

Kenya has some large ▶ cities but it has a lot of countryside, too.

Meet Ronnie

Ronnie is eight years old. He lives in a house in Nairobi. Ronnie lives with his mother, father, and baby sister, Connie.

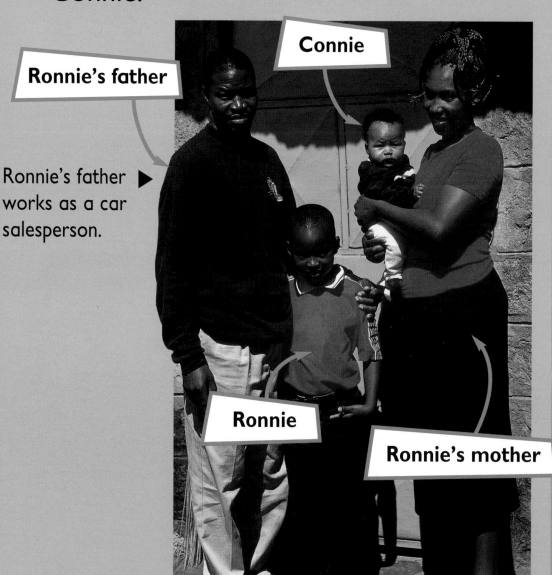

Ronnie's father ▶ works as a car salesperson.

Ronnie's father

Connie

Ronnie

Ronnie's mother

▲ Ronnie's family eats breakfast together every morning.

Ronnie's mother stays at home to take care of Connie. Ronnie helps his mother at home. He keeps his room clean, and he helps take care of Connie.

Ronnie's School

Ronnie goes to school five days a week. He studies math, English, art, **Swahili**, citizenship, religion, and the **environment**. He likes art best.

▲ There are 35 children in Ronnie's class. They have their lessons in Swahili.

At lunch time, Ronnie and his friends play on the playground. There are swings and a climbing frame. They can play soccer, too.

Ronnie's class eats ▶ their lunch in the classroom.

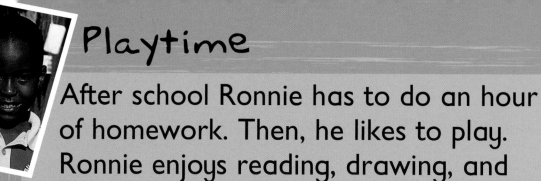

Playtime

After school Ronnie has to do an hour of homework. Then, he likes to play. Ronnie enjoys reading, drawing, and watching television. He likes to ride his bike, too.

◀ Ronnie and his friends play outside on the street.

Ronnie likes to play ▶ on the swings at the school playground.

Ronnie's best friends are Lillian and Joseph. They play together at home and at school. They like playing at school because there is a big playground.

11

Farming and Fishing

Kenya has a lot of different farms. The high land in the center of Kenya is good for growing plants. Tea and coffee are grown in Kenya and sold all over the world.

Many people grow and ▶ pick tea in Kenya.

fish

Some people grow fruit, vegetables, and rice to sell at the markets. Some sell flowers that they grow. Fishers work on Lake Victoria and sell the fish they catch.

Meet Grace

Grace is seven years old. She lives in Mwea, a small village in the middle of Kenya. Grace lives with her mother, father, brother, and two sisters.

▼ Everyone in Mwea knows each other.

Grace's father

Grace's mother

Grace

Grace's brother

Grace's sisters

▲ Grace has lots of space to play outside. She likes playing jump rope.

Grace's house has no water or **electricity**. Her family get water from a stream. They use wood to make a fire for cooking food on.

15

Grace's Work

Grace goes to school for five days a week. She likes going to school because she has a lot of friends there. When she grows up, Grace wants to be a teacher.

Grace and her ▶ friends work hard at school.

After school, Grace does her homework. Then she helps her parents. She collects firewood for cooking with and carries water from the stream.

Grace's main job ▶ is to take care of the goats.

Food

Grace's parents are farmers. They grow rice to eat and to sell at the market in Mwea. With the money they make at the market, they buy cabbages, potatoes, or tomatoes.

Most farming ▶ in Kenya is done by hand.

18

For a special treat, Grace's parents buy beef to eat. Grace's favorite food is rice and beans, but she likes it best with beef!

Grace likes to help ▶ her mother sort beans for cooking.

Market Day

Markets are very important in Kenya. People go to markets to buy and sell food and clothes.

Market day is always very busy. ▶

▲ In some places, people dress in **traditional** clothes or jewelery for market day.

People also go to the market to meet their friends and talk. Most Kenyans buy their clothes from clothes markets.

Meet Betty and Naomi

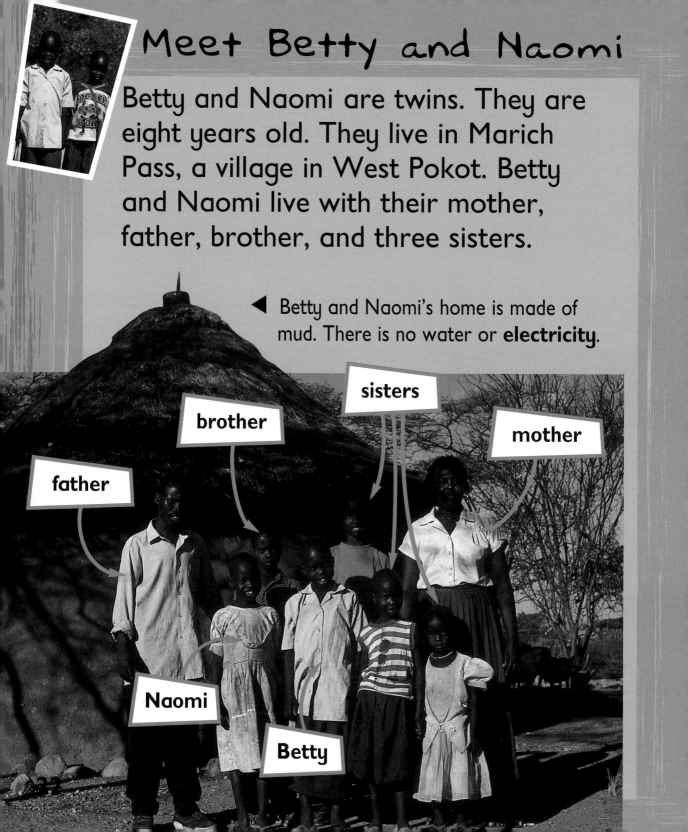

Betty and Naomi are twins. They are eight years old. They live in Marich Pass, a village in West Pokot. Betty and Naomi live with their mother, father, brother, and three sisters.

◀ Betty and Naomi's home is made of mud. There is no water or **electricity**.

sisters

brother

mother

father

Naomi

Betty

▲ West Pokot often has **droughts**.

West Pokot is very dry. The family gets water from the river. Sometimes there is not enough rain for them to grow food. They have to rely on **charities** to bring them food.

At School

Betty and Naomi go to school five days a week. School for young children is free in Kenya. But the family will have to sell some goats to pay for the twins to go to school when they are older.

Betty and Naomi live ▶ close to school so they can walk there.

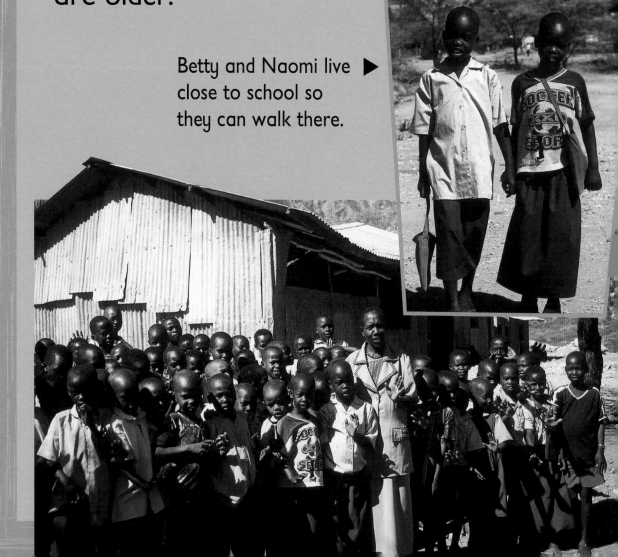

At school, the children sit on the floor for lessons because there are no desks. Betty and Naomi study English, **Swahili**, math, history, science, and art. They like math best.

◀ At recess. the children like to play soccer or basketball.

25

Work

After school, the twins do their homework. They have jobs to do at home, too. They care for the goats and collect firewood. They help cook and clean.

▼ Betty and Naomi help carry water from the river twice a day.

Betty and Naomi's ► mother runs the local shop.

Betty and Naomi help take care of their little sister because their parents work. Their father teaches at the nursery school. He also shows **tourists** around.

Tourism

Tourists come to Kenya to see its beautiful mountains and beaches. A lot of people in Kenya work by helping **tourists**. They show tourists around, work as drivers, or work in hotels.

◀ There are many large hotels in Kenya for tourists to stay in.

▼ Tourists on a safari can see animals living in the wild.

Many tourists come to Kenya to see the animals that live there. They go on a **safari**. They can see lions, elephants, zebras, hippos, and leopards.

Kenyan Fact File

Flag   **Capital city**   **Money**

Nairobi

Kenyan shilling

Religion
• Most people in Kenya are Christians. There are some Muslims, too.

Language
• English and **Swahili** are the official languages of Kenya. There are many tribal languages as well.

Try speaking Swahili!
Jambo! .... *Hello!*
Hujambo?....................................... *How are you?*
Asante .... *Thank you.*

Glossary

charity group that helps people who are poor or in need

drought dry weather and no rain for a long time

electricity power used for heating, lighting, and making machines work

environment the natural world in which people, plants, and animals live

safari journey to see wild animals

Swahili official language of Kenya

tourist someone who is visiting on vacation

traditional something that has been going on for a very long time without changing

tropical hot and muggy, with lots of rain

More Books to Read

Auch, Alison. *Welcome to Kenya*. Minneapolis, Minn.: Compass Point Books, 2002.

Fontes, Justine and Ron Fontes. *A to Z Kenya*. Danbury, Conn.: Children's Press, 2004

Raatma, Lucia. *Kenya*. Minneapolis, Minn.: Compass Point Books, 2002.

Index